First Facts®

easy origami

EASY SPACE
Origami

by Christopher L. Harbo

CAPSTONE PRESS
a capstone imprint

First Facts is published by Capstone Press,
1710 Roe Crest Drive, North Mankato, Minnesota 56003.
www.capstonepub.com

 Books published by Capstone Press are manufactured with paper
containing at least 10 percent post-consumer waste.

Library of Congress Cataloging-in-Publication Data
Harbo, Christopher L.
  Easy space origami / by Christopher L. Harbo.
    p. cm.—(First facts. Easy origami)
  Includes bibliographical references.
  ISBN 978-1-4296-6001-3 (library binding)
  1. Origami—Juvenile literature. 2. Space vehicles in art—Juvenile literature. I. Title. II. Series.

TT870.H323 2012
736'.982—dc22   2011001011

Summary: Provides instructions and photo-illustrated diagrams for making a variety of easy
space-related origami models.

Editorial Credits
Designer: GENE BENTDAHL
Photo Studio Specialist: SARAH SCHUETTE
Scheduler: MARCY MORIN
Production Specialist: LAURA MANTHE

Photo Credits
Capstone Studio/Karon Dubke, all photos

Artistic Effects
Nova Development Corporation

ABOUT THE AUTHOR

Christopher L. Harbo loves origami. He began folding
paper several years ago and hasn't quit since. In
addition to decorative origami, he also enjoys folding
paper airplanes. When he's not practicing origami,
Christopher spends his free time reading Japanese
comic books and watching movies.

Printed in the United States of America in North Mankato, Minnesota.
112012   006976R

TABLE OF Contents

ORIGAMI Adventure

Explore the universe one fold at a time. Inside this book you'll discover seven easy models that have to do with outer space. Turn a simple ribbon into a shining star. Use a puff of air to make a moon lander. Test your folding skills on a green martian. Every project will let your imagination soar. Blast off on an origami adventure that's out of this world!

MATERIALS

Origami is a simple art that doesn't use many materials. You'll only need the following things to complete the projects in this book:

Origami Paper: Square origami paper comes in many fun colors and sizes. You can buy this paper in most craft stores.

Ruler: Some models use measurements to complete. A ruler will help you measure.

Scissors: Sometimes a model needs a snip here or there to complete. Keep a scissors nearby.

Pencil: Use a pencil when you need to mark spots you measure with the ruler.

Craft Supplies: Markers and other craft supplies will help you decorate your models.

FOLDING TECHNIQUES

Folding paper is easier when you understand basic origami folds and symbols. Practice the folds on this list before trying the models in this book. Turn back to this list if you get stuck on a tricky step, or ask an adult for help.

Valley Folds are represented by a dashed line. One side of the paper is folded against the other like a book. A sharp fold is made by running your finger along the fold line.

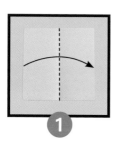

Mountain Folds are represented by a pink or white dashed and dotted line. The paper is folded sharply behind the model.

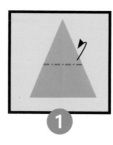

Squash Folds are formed by lifting one edge of a pocket. The pocket gets folded again so the spine gets flattened. The existing fold lines become new edges.

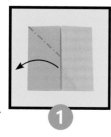

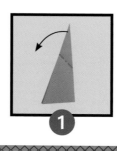

Inside reverse folds are made by opening a pocket slightly. Then you fold the model inside itself along existing fold lines.

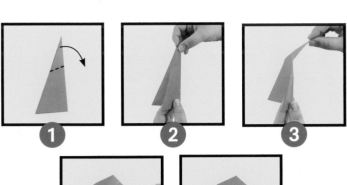

Outside reverse folds are made by opening a pocket slightly. Then you fold the model outside itself along existing fold lines.

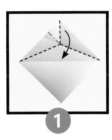

Rabbit ear folds are formed by bringing two edges of a point together using existing fold lines. The new point is folded to one side.

SYMBOLS

SINGLE-POINTED ARROW:
Fold the paper in the direction of the arrow.

DOUBLE-POINTED ARROW:
Fold the paper and then unfold it.

HALF-POINTED ARROW:
Fold the paper behind.

LOOPING ARROW:
Turn the paper over or turn it to a new position.

STRIPED ARROW:
Blow into the model to puff it up.

GALACTIC Ring

Traditional Model

Every astronaut needs a cool ride. Soar through the air with this ring-shaped ship.

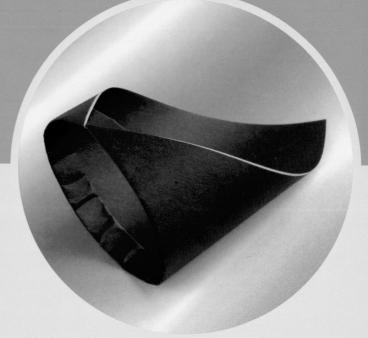

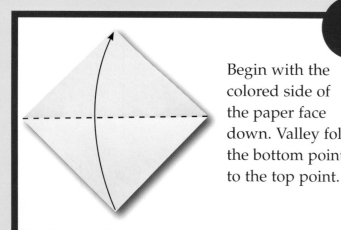

1 Begin with the colored side of the paper face down. Valley fold the bottom point to the top point.

2 Valley fold the bottom edge to make a narrow strip.

3 Valley fold the bottom edge again.

4

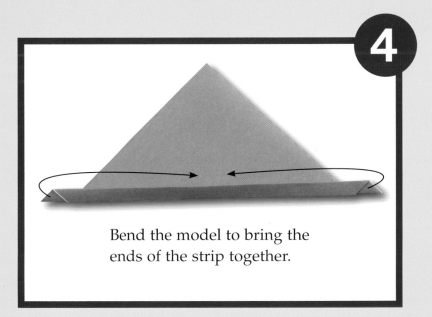

Bend the model to bring the ends of the strip together.

5

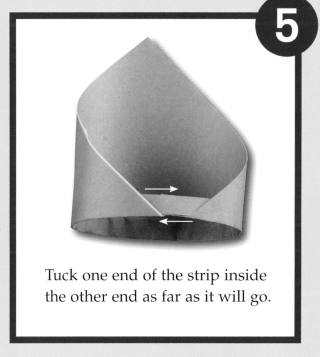

Tuck one end of the strip inside the other end as far as it will go.

6

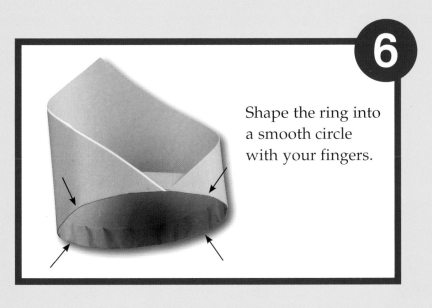

Shape the ring into a smooth circle with your fingers.

7

Send your galactic ring soaring.

FLIGHT Tip Hold the pointed end of the ring with your index finger and thumb. Release the galactic ring with a gentle forward push. Hold it high when you launch it to make it glide farther.

SHINING Star

Traditional Model

Make amazing little stars with long, thin ribbons of paper. Use a foil paper to really help them shine.

1

Cut a 0.5 inch (1.3 centimeter) strip off one side of a 10 inch (25 cm) square of paper.

2

Start with the colored side of the strip face down. Tie the left end of the strip into a knot. Carefully tighten the knot.

3

Valley fold the short strip on the left side of the knot. Tuck the strip under the top layer of the knot.

4

Valley fold the long strip across the knot. The strip will overlap the edge opposite your fold.

5

Mountain fold the long strip behind the knot. Note how the strip comes up behind the edge opposite your fold.

6

Continue making valley and mountain folds to wrap the strip around the knot. Stop folding when you have only a short strip left.

7

Valley fold the short strip. Tuck the strip under the top layer of the knot.

8

Hold the edges of the knot between your fingers and thumbs. Use a fingernail to gently press in each side of the knot. Note how the indented edges cause the middle of the knot to puff up.

9

Your star is shining!

SECRET TIP String dozens of stars together with a needle and thread. Then decorate your room by hanging your string of shining stars around a window or door frame.

GLIDING Spaceship

Based on a model by Makoto Yamaguchi

Get ready to skim across the surface of a distant planet. This clever spaceship glides smoothly with a blast of air.

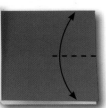

1 Start with the colored side of the paper face down. Valley fold the top edge to the bottom edge.

2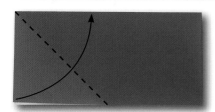

Valley fold the bottom-left corner of the top layer to the top edge.

3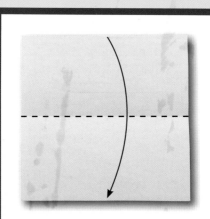

Mountain fold the bottom-left corner of the bottom layer to the top edge.

4

Grab the bottom edge of the top layer and pull it up to the top edge. Make a short valley fold on the right edge and unfold.

5

Valley fold the top-right corner and unfold. Note how the fold runs from the triangle flap to the fold made in step 4.

6

Inside reverse fold on the fold from step 5. This fold allows the top-right corner to tuck inside the model.

7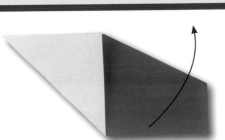

Lift the top flap of the model.

8

Valley fold the hidden triangle up as far as it will go. Lower the top flap.

9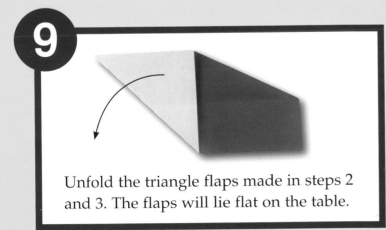

Unfold the triangle flaps made in steps 2 and 3. The flaps will lie flat on the table.

10

The spaceship is ready to glide.

 PLAY TIP Set the spaceship on a table. Gently blow into the back of the model. Watch your spaceship glide.

MOON Lander

Traditional Model

Take a trip to the moon. This tiny pod looks like the first moon landers astronauts used.

1

Begin with the colored side of the paper face up. Valley fold the top edge to the bottom edge and unfold. Valley fold the left edge to the right edge and unfold.

2

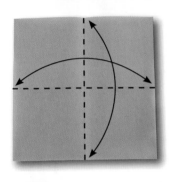

Turn the paper over.

3

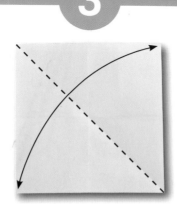

Valley fold the bottom-left corner to the top-right corner. Make a firm fold and unfold.

4

Valley fold the top-left corner to the bottom right corner.

14

5

Squash fold by grabbing the top-right corner of the paper. Pull the corner down to the left on the existing folds. Flatten the paper into a triangle.

6

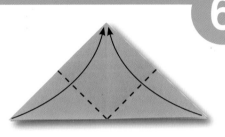

Valley fold the left and right points of the top layer to the center fold. Repeat this step on the back side of the model.

7

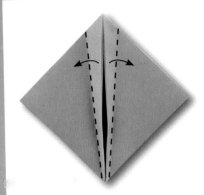

Valley fold the center edges of the top layer outward. Note how the folds meet the bottom point. Repeat this step on the back side of the model.

8

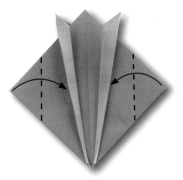

Valley fold the left and right points of the top layer. Tuck them under the flaps made in step 7. Repeat this step on the back side of the model.

9

Spread the sides of the model apart slightly. Blow air into the hole at the bottom of the model. The model will puff up to form a cube with legs.

10

Pretend your lander has touched down on the moon.

SECRET Tip The moon lander can also serve as a bug cage. Ladybugs and other small beetles can fit through the hole in the model's top.

15

WINGED Cap

Traditional Model

You can't explore space without the right hat. This winged cap will get your imagination soaring among the stars.

1

Begin with the colored side of the paper face up. Valley fold the top point to the bottom point and unfold. Valley fold the left point to the right point and unfold.

2

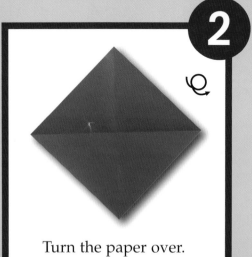

Turn the paper over.

3

Valley fold the bottom-left edge to the top-right edge and unfold.

4

Valley fold the top-left edge to the bottom-right edge.

5

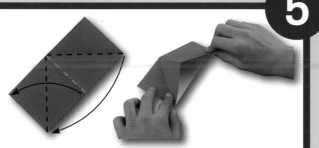

Squash fold by lifting the top-right corner of the paper. Pull the corner down to the left on the existing folds. Flatten the paper into a square shape.

6

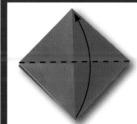

Valley fold the bottom point of the top layer. Repeat this step on the back side of the model.

7

Valley fold the left point of the top layer. Repeat this step on the back side of the model.

8

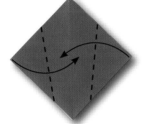

Valley fold the top layer's left and right points. Note that the points cross the center fold and overlap. Repeat this step on the back side of the model.

9

Valley fold the bottom point of the top layer to the top point. Repeat this step on the back side of the model.

10

Mountain fold the top flap's point. Tuck the point into the pocket behind the flap. Repeat this step on the back side of the model.

11

Open the bottom of the model, and carefully pull the sides apart.

12

Soar into space with your winged cap!

SECRET Tip

To wear the winged cap, fold a piece of paper large enough to fit your head. An 18-inch (46-cm) square of newspaper works well.

SPACE PIRATE Boots

Traditional Model

Traveling in space isn't all about speedy spaceships. Space pirates need a good pair of pointy boots to carry them across the galaxy.

1

Use a scissors to cut a square piece of paper in half.

2

Begin with one of the halves colored side face down. Valley fold the bottom edge to the top edge.

3

Valley fold the left edge to the right edge and unfold.

4

Valley fold the bottom-left edge to the center fold. Valley fold the bottom-right edge to the center fold.

5

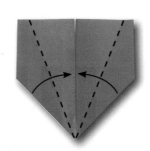

Valley fold the bottom-left edge to the center fold. Valley fold the bottom-right edge to the center fold.

6

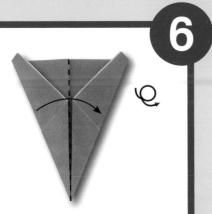

Valley fold the left edge to the right edge. Then turn the model so the point faces to the left.

7

Valley fold the top layer's bottom edge. Note how the bottom edge meets the slanting edge near the middle of the model.

8

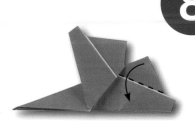

Valley fold the bottom layer's triangle along the slanting edge.

9

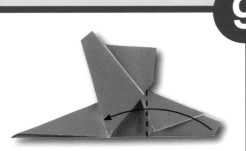

Valley fold the bottom layer to the left. Tuck the layer into the pocket of the boot's toe.

10

Valley fold the left flap even with the top of the boot.

11

Mountain fold the small triangle. Tuck it into the pocket on the upper part of the boot.

12

Your finished boot is ready to stand. Make a second boot for a matching pair.

SECRET Tip

The space pirate boots can also be made using dollar bills.

GREEN Martian

Traditional Model

Everyone knows martians are green, right? This little guy even has four arms and a spacesuit!

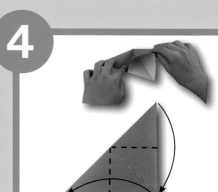

1 Start with the colored side of the paper face up. Valley fold the bottom edge to the top edge and unfold. Valley fold the left edge to the right edge and unfold. Turn the paper over.

2 Valley fold the bottom-left corner to the top-right corner and unfold.

3 Valley fold the top-left corner down to the bottom-right corner.

4 Squash fold by grabbing the paper's top-right corner. Pull the corner down to the left on the existing folds. Flatten the paper into a triangle.

5

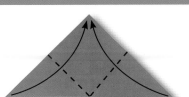

Valley fold the bottom edges of the top layer to the center fold. Repeat this step on the back side of the model.

6

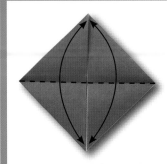

Valley fold both top points to the bottom point and unfold. Repeat this step on the back side of the model.

7

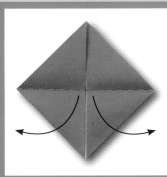

Squash fold both top flaps on the folds made in step 6. The flaps will flatten into squares. Repeat this step on the back side of the model.

8

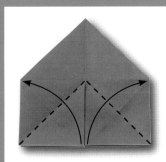

Valley fold both bottom-inside corners to the outside corners. Repeat this step on the back side of the model.

9

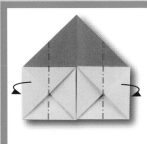

Mountain fold the left side of the top flap inside the model. Mountain fold the right side of the top flap inside the model. Repeat both of these folds on the back side of the model.

10

Valley fold the bottom point to the center edge. Repeat this step on the back side of the model.

11

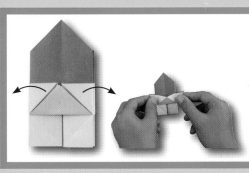

Pinch the triangles along the center edge of the model. Pull them out gently to form two arms. Then repeat this step on the back side of the model.

12

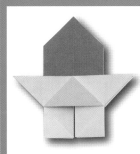

Draw a face for your little green man.

SECRET Tip Bend the martian's arms toward you to make it look more lifelike.

Origami
SPACE ADVENTURE

READ More

Boursin, Didier. *Folding for Fun.* Richmond Hill, Ont.: Firefly Books, 2007.

Engel, Peter. *10-Fold Origami: Fabulous Paperfolds You Can Make in 10 Steps or Less.* New York: Sterling Pub. Co., Inc., 2008.

Harbo, Christopher L. *Easy Ocean Origami.* Easy Origami. Mankato, Minn.: Capstone Press, 2011.

Meinking, Mary. *Easy Origami.* Origami. Mankato, Minn.: Capstone Press, 2009.

INTERNET Sites

FactHound offers a safe, fun way to find Internet sites related to this book. All of the sites on FactHound have been researched by our staff.

Here's all you do:

Visit *www.facthound.com*

Type in this code: 9781429660013

Super-cool stuff! Check out projects, games and lots more at www.capstonekids.com